Mindful Journaling

Mindful Journaling

Tara Ward

ARCTURUS

ARCTURUS

This edition published in 2019 by Arcturus Publishing Limited
26/27 Bickels Yard, 151–153 Bermondsey Street,
London SE1 3HA

ISBN: 978-1-78428-364-3
AD005254US

Printed in China

Contents

Author's Note

Have you noticed how we seem to spend a lot of our life working toward specific goals: to be the best child, adult, partner, parent, work colleague, or leader in our field that we can be? We tend to focus on the goal itself and yet, if we reach it, the victory can feel unsatisfying. If we don't fulfill our goals, then we are doubly discouraged.

A full and contented life is one experienced moment by moment. Adopting mindful techniques makes the journey itself the true joy and the end result less significant. Our satisfaction comes from HOW we live our life, not what we do or don't accomplish along the way.

This is what mindfulness has taught me.

INTRODUCTION

MINDFULNESS ITSELF IS EASY.
REMEMBERING TO BE MINDFUL IS THE CHALLENGE.

WHY KEEP A MINDFUL JOURNAL?

Mindfulness—"being in the moment"—is a great way to live and, like everything you want to accomplish, the more you practice, the better you become. Keeping a journal of your mindful experiences will help you appreciate how useful they are and will encourage you to try all the different suggestions offered here.

HOW TO USE IT

I've created this mindful journal to be fun and inspiring so, once you have read through the Introduction, you don't have to start at the beginning—unless you want to. You can scroll through until a suggestion appeals, pick your favorite number, and see what is on that page, choose your favorite color and go to a page in that section, or even close your eyes and choose a page at random!

Sometimes, you might want to take a while to enjoy a mindful activity; on other occasions it could be fleeting. You may have the urge to write down your thoughts in detail or just scribble one or two sentences. Some suggestions may resonate powerfully with you and others less so. If you can't connect with an idea, simply leave it and come back to it later.

Most of us are busy with our daily lives, so don't worry if your visits are not as frequent as you'd like. Having said that, mindfulness is most pleasurable when it becomes a habit, so if you can delve into your journal at least once or twice a week, it will help you to enjoy it more fully. And remember, many of my suggestions take only a few moments.

Before you leap in, let's look at what mindfulness means, how it can benefit you, and a few helpful hints to make this journal really useful for you.

WHAT IS MINDFULNESS?

Put simply, mindfulness is about being "in the now," focusing on what is happening in any given moment, including how you feel. The reason this is so important is because most of us spend a lot of our time thinking either about the past or the future, in other words we reflect upon what has happened to us already or we concern ourselves greatly with what is, or might be, coming up.

As children we were better at being mindful, but as adulthood looms with its responsibilities and challenges, most of us lose the capacity. The good news is that discovering it again is great fun!

HOW DOES MINDFULNESS HELP YOU?

If you are going to invest some time in experiencing mindfulness, it would be good to know what the benefits are—and there are many.

Mindfulness helps you to enjoy life in every way, from eating and sleeping to playing and working. When you are mindful of what you are doing, you can appreciate everything more. Since discovering mindfulness, I have smiled a lot!

It gives you the ability to understand yourself better, including emotionally, and to change unhelpful patterns of behavior into useful ones.

This has been verified by cognitive neuroscientists who confirm that mindfulness activities can change brain activity in the areas that control well-being and process emotion. Positive links have also been discovered with reducing stress hormones and strengthening the immune system.

These are just a few benefits of mindfulness; you will discover many more as you explore this journal.

A FEW DOS AND DON'TS BEFORE YOU START

- As with every form of self-development, there are a few provisos. You should avoid using the journal if taking mind-altering drugs or alcohol.

- If you feel particularly low, you might want to consider whether delving into your emotions at this time is right for you. It may be very helpful, but make sure you choose the right mindful exercise for your frame of mind.

- Most suggestions are structured around being on your own, so don't try them when you are responsible for people in your care.

- Lastly, awareness of breath is a big part of mindfulness, so it is always helpful to focus on your breathing for a moment or two before you start. Also, occasionally you may have emotions or feelings you want to wash away.

- So just before you jump forward, here are two very useful exercises you may want to use a lot: one to help your awareness of breath and one to use as a cleanser if you need to wash away anything before, during, or after.

Breathing exercise

Sit or stand comfortably with your weight on both feet. Start to become aware of your breathing without trying to alter it in any way. Notice the air coming in through your nostrils or mouth and making its way down into your lungs. Feel your lungs expand and then deflate as the air comes back, up and out through your nose or mouth. Repeat the awareness a few times. You will realize some breaths are deeper, some more shallow. This is normal. Don't try to change it in any way; just observe it and enjoy it. Allow yourself as much time as possible to do this. After a while, you may notice that your breaths deepen naturally without any effort. Become aware of how heavy both your feet feel on the ground before you continue.

Cleansing exercise

* If possible, sit with both feet resting equally balanced on the floor. Close your eyes. Otherwise, stand with your weight firmly on both feet and keep your eyes open, but soften your vision so you are not staring at anything in particular.

* Now imagine you are under a beautiful waterfall or shower and the water is gushing over you, cleansing away any unwanted feelings.

* Spend time visualizing your surroundings: what they look, sound, smell, and feel like. What is under your bare feet? What are the colors around you? The textures? What can you hear? What do you smell?

* Take your time and enjoy the feeling of being cleansed. When you are ready, let the image of the waterfall or shower fade, and make sure your feet feel nice and solid on the floor before you continue your day.

* Remember, you can use these two exercises at any time during your mindful exercises. Some of my suggestions are lighthearted; others may encourage you to delve deeper into your emotions. So choose whatever is right for you at the time.

* Right. When you are ready, turn the page and get started!

ONE

WHEN YOU WAKE IN THE MORNING, LIE STILL FOR A MOMENT
BEFORE YOU OPEN YOUR EYES.

What can you hear?

How does the bed linen feel against your skin? What thoughts are running through your mind as you wake up? How do those thoughts nurture you? If they aren't helpful, how could you change them? Focus on your breathing before you start your day. You might want to wait until later before writing down your thoughts upon waking.

THE NEXT TIME YOU GO FOOD SHOPPING, STAND IN FRONT OF THE FRUIT/VEGETABLE SECTION AND LOOK CLOSELY AT WHAT IS ON OFFER.

What are you naturally drawn to?

What colors appeal? Why? What can you smell the most as you stand in front of it all? Pick up a piece and hold it in your hand. How do you feel about it? Do you want to buy it or do you want to put it back? Why? Continue the rest of your shopping, really focusing on items before you choose them. Reflect on how you choose the products of nature, and the benefits they bring.

STAND WITH YOUR WEIGHT DISTRIBUTED EVENLY ON BOTH FEET.

Hold on to something to keep you steady. Slowly roll your weight along each part of your feet, starting with your heels and working your way along your soles and right up onto your toes. Then roll back again to your heels. Repeat. Notice how you feel the stretch in parts of your legs and how you can feel more parts of your feet with each slow roll. Finish by putting both feet back flat on the ground and appreciate how you feel now. This will help to "ground you" and bring your attention mindfully back to your body in less than a minute. Can you imagine the benefits of devoting time to yourself like this? How does it make you feel?

EXPLORE WHERE YOUR THOUGHTS TAKE YOU WHEN YOU DON'T TRY TO CONTROL THEM.

Commit to five minutes when you won't be disturbed. Sit or lie somewhere you feel comfortable. Close your eyes and feel your breath coming into and out of your body. Observe your first thought, without controlling it in any way. Imagine it as a cloud that floats by. Let it go, without attaching any meaning or significance to it. Wait to see what thought comes next without trying to steer your mind in any direction. Again, let it float by, without analyzing it. Repeat this for as long as you feel comfortable, maintaining a pleasant detachment from your thoughts. Make notes afterward about your thoughts and how you felt by trying to detach from them as much as possible. When would it be useful to do this during the day?

Take your time, exploring each ridge and crevice. Notice the different textures and how some areas are particularly sensitive. As you do this, consider what your face says about you to other people. Is it a reflection of who you truly are or do you "put on a different face" to the world? Become aware of your emotions. Pat your face very gently when you finish and give thanks for it. What have you learned about yourself?

MAKE YOURSELF A DRINK

Before you sip it, cup your hands around the container. What is the temperature of the drink? How does that make you feel? What does it smell like? What do you think about the color? Take a small sip and hold it in your mouth before you swallow it. What does it taste like? Where in your mouth could you feel it? As you swallow, feel the liquid running down through your throat and into your body. How far can you feel it? (If you repeat this, you will realize you can feel more of the drink's journey each time.) Now you have done this, record how this drink makes you feel. How satisfied do you feel from it? Is there anything you might enjoy more? Why?

LOOK AT WHAT IS AROUND YOU RIGHT NOW.

Choose one object to focus upon.

What made you choose that item? Really look at it, study it closely. What appeals/doesn't appeal? What does it mean to you? Notice what emotions surface for you. Cleanse away anything you don't want. Think about where it has come from and what it is doing there now. Engage in any way possible with the item, such as smelling, touching, tasting, drawing it, or noting down any sound it makes—observe and record how it makes you feel.

WHERE DOES THE WORD "PEACE" LIVE INSIDE OF YOU?

Close your eyes and say the word "peace" to yourself.

Breathe deeply and comfortably. Notice where your attention is drawn to in your body. Why this spot? What does it mean to you? Focus all your attention on this spot and breathe into it. How is it making you feel now? Notice how heavy your feet feel on the ground before you open your eyes and continue your day. Don't be surprised if you find yourself feeling calm for quite a while afterward! Write down what you experience, and repeat the exercise when you can.

WALK INTO A PARK AND FIND A QUIET SPOT TO STOP.
OBSERVE WHAT IS IMMEDIATELY AROUND YOU.

What attracts you the most and why?

Look at all the different colors and textures. Touch something. How does it make you feel? Smell something. What does that scent make you think and feel? As you breathe in, imagine you are breathing in the energy of nature around you. Notice your emotions. Write them down when you have a moment to yourself.

WRITE THE WORD "MINDFUL" ON A PIECE OF PAPER AND LOOK AT IT.

What does it mean to you?

What do you feel about the word? What other words are within it? Trace the word with your finger and notice how you feel. Then write the word in different ways on separate sheets of paper. Spread out the different styles in front of you and study them. What do they represent to you? Make notes about how you feel against each.

LET OUT A LONG, LOW "AAH" SOUND, RELAXING YOUR JAW
AS YOU DO SO. FEEL THE VIBRATION OF YOUR SOUND THROUGH YOUR BODY.

Where do you sense it most?

How does it make you feel? Let out another "aah," either louder or softer in volume. What is the difference in sensation? How does focusing on your own voice make you feel? Change the sound to "ooh" and notice how you feel. Play with different sounds and write down how they make you feel.

See how many different colors there are on your hand. Look at the shape of it and realize how complex it is, made up of many muscles, bones, tendons, ligaments, and veins. Think about the tasks your hand does every day. Stroke your hand gently. Smell it. Give thanks for it. Record how you feel about your hand after this. You might even want to make a list of all the things your hand does each day.

This sounds odd, doesn't it?

But most of us always use the same foot first as we go up and down stairs. Notice what you do and then switch to start off on your other foot. It may feel odd and that's fine. It is your brain acknowledging that something feels different. It's easier to be mindful when something jolts you into connecting with your body again. Please remember to hold onto those bannisters because it can make you feel unbalanced initially. Doing something in a new way helps strengthen our connections between mind and body. Write down how you felt.

PLACE SOMETHING YOU'D LIKE TO EAT IN FRONT OF YOU.
LOOK AT IT CLOSELY.

Where has it come from?

Who or what was involved in its journey from conception to where it is now in front of you? Really reflect upon the steps/stages involved. How do you feel about the food now as you think about its past? Consider whom you would like to thank and thank them silently. Feel grateful for their contribution. Then, if you feel like it, slowly eat the food, taking small bites and really savoring the taste and texture. How could this experience change how you eat in future? Write down your thoughts so that you remember them.

Close your eyes and focus on your breathing. After a while, you may notice a light, fluttering sensation on your fingertips or forehead. Breathe and allow yourself to experience whatever is happening. There may be images or feelings that come up. Observe them without trying to understand them. If there is anything you don't like, wash it away using the Cleansing Exercise (page 9). When you are ready, take your fingers away from your forehead and cleanse properly with your waterfall/shower. Make sure your feet feel heavy on the floor before you open your eyes, then write down your thoughts.

Read the quote below from Lao Tzu.

How does it make you feel? Where do you spend most of your time?

What would it take for you to live more in the present?

If you are depressed, you are living in the past.
If you are anxious, you are living in the future.
If you are at peace, you are living in the present.

PICK A BLADE OF GRASS OR A LEAF AND SIT WITH IT IN YOUR HANDS. STUDY ITS SHAPE, COLOR, AND NOTICE ANY IRREGULARITIES.

Let it slide through your fingers and then sniff it. As you do this, be aware of what you are feeling, what you are thinking. Let this blade of grass or leaf become your sole focus. Notice how beautiful it is. Reflect on different aspects of it: its strength and weakness; how prolific it is; where it grows; how it grows; what animals and humans do with it. (It's fine if, at the end, you find it hard to throw away the blade of grass or leaf. You might even want to tape it inside your journal!)

Let yourself react physically if you wish. Imagine the music swirling around you and seeping into your bones. What are you experiencing right now? How does your body feel? Where in your body do you feel the music the most? What does that mean to you? How would different music affect you? Make a note of anything you want to. Remember you have your waterfall/shower exercise to wash away anything you don't wish to retain.

RINSE A WASHCLOTH UNDER HOT WATER AND PLACE IT GENTLY OVER YOUR FACE.

Let the warmth seep into your skin and take time to enjoy the sensation. How does that make you feel? Repeat with cold water. What is the difference in your emotions? Which do you prefer? Why? Notice how your face feels afterward and how that affects all of you. Record any reflections that occur to you.

SPEND ONE DAY WHEN YOU CHALLENGE EVERY ASSUMPTION YOU MAKE.

Whenever you feel an assumption coming into your mind (it can be something simple such as "I don't like that" or "I bet he/she is difficult"), stop and ask yourself why you are thinking that way. Where does that attitude stem from? What could you do to change it? After just one day, you will discover how many assumptions you make, all day, without realizing it. How would it benefit you to change some of them? Write down the assumptions you make most often and place some suggestions on how to change your attitude against each one.

What is your first response to saying this?

Think about why you feel this way. Now ask yourself where you could be more mindful. How can you incorporate it into your day without it being an effort? When do you most enjoy mindful activity? When are you most likely to forget? What gets in the way of mindfulness? How can you overcome that? What do you most want to achieve through being more mindful? Make notes to remind yourself. Then repeat the experience and notice the differences as you increase your mindful moments.

LOOK AT A PERSONAL PHOTO YOU ARE DRAWN TO AND FOCUS ON IT.

Notice what emotions come over you as you do this. If you concentrate fully, memories may surface and surprise you. Let them come. They may include scents, sounds, taste, and the touch of something, or a memory you had completely forgotten. Notice what you are feeling and thinking without trying to control it in any way. Cleanse away anything you don't want to hold onto. The more you focus on the photo, the more you are likely to become drawn into it, and the more you will feel. Stop when you have had enough and put away the photo before you write down your feelings. Notice whether you want to have that photo around you more as a result—or if you feel less drawn to it.

Feel your lungs expanding and contracting. Now imagine that your lungs, instead of being behind your rib cage, are actually way down in your buttocks. Imagine breathing into them! It's fine if that makes you smile or laugh. The thought process alone will automatically deepen your breaths without it being a conscious effort. Enjoy the sensation. Make sure your feet feel heavy on the ground before you stand. Write down how you felt.

LOOK AT A COLOR CHART. YOU COULD FIND ONE ONLINE OR PICK UP
A PAINT CHART FROM YOUR LOCAL HARDWARE STORE. LET YOUR EYES SWEEP OVER
THE COLORS AND STOP WHEN YOU ARE DRAWN TO ONE IN PARTICULAR.

Why are you drawn to it?

What does it mean to you and how does it make you feel? Then, if you
are comfortable, imagine the color is coming into you as you breathe in. Use
your breath to breathe out the color, or imagine the color spreading through
your body if you wish. Feel the effect of the color and wash it away when
you have had enough. Experiment with different colors when you have time.
Notice how they make you feel. You may find scents, sounds, images, or
tastes attach themselves to individual colors. What colors are you most drawn
to? What do you avoid? Why? Makes notes and see if your relationship to
colors changes over time.

THINK OF ONE THING FOR WHICH YOU ARE GRATEFUL. ALLOW THE
FEELING OF GRATITUDE TO SWEEP OVER AND THROUGH YOU. FOCUS ON
WHY YOU FEEL THAT WAY.

Notice how it makes you feel. Work out where it manifests itself in your body and what that feeling is like. Let your appreciation swell even more until it fills all of you. Have that feeling stay with you for as long as you can through the day. Notice when something happens that diminishes it and counteract that effect by focusing again on your gratitude. Make notes about where this gratitude resides in you and play with other words to discover where they live in you.

AS YOU WASH/RINSE YOUR DISHES, REFLECT ON THE PRIVILEGE OF
HAVING RUNNING WATER, BOTH HOT AND COLD.

Become sensitive to the flow of water and how wonderful it is. Give thanks
for clean water and the physical ability to do this task. You may wish to
appreciate the meal you have eaten or the people with whom you shared it.
Instead of rushing the task, clean/rinse the dishes slowly and feel gratitude.
When you finish, reflect on what you experienced and how it has left you
feeling. Note down your thoughts.

BODY AWARENESS 1:

Give a long, slow stretch.

You can be standing, sitting, or lying. Take your time and appreciate the sensation of your body lengthening. Notice where your body feels comfortable as you stretch. Observe where it feels tighter and is less yielding. As you relax back from the stretch, check how you feel. You may be more aware of certain parts of your body now. Take a second slow, gentle stretch. Do some areas feel even more relaxed? Is there any area that still feels uncomfortable? Stretch for a third time, still being very slow and careful. Write down what you have learned from this exercise. Then if you still feel tension in parts of your body, try the exercise on the next page...

BODY AWARENESS 2:

Focus on the area of your body that feels tense or uncomfortable.

What is it trying to tell you? Why does it feel this way? Ask the area what you need to do to make it more comfortable. How can you nurture it better in future? Then, take a deep breath in and, as you breathe out, imagine the breath going directly to the area that is uncomfortable. As it does so, the part of your body that is in discomfort may relax a little. Repeat this action several times, noticing how it feels. It might help you to touch gently the area that is affected since that can help focus the breath. Stop when you have had enough. Remember what your body told you it needed to help alleviate tension by writing it down.

MINDFUL MEALS

Eat your next meal slowly and carefully.

Savor all the scents, tastes, and textures. Chew thoroughly before you swallow. Halfway through your meal, stop and focus on your stomach. How full is it feeling? How much are you enjoying the food? Notice when you have had enough, irrespective of whether you have finished your meal. Repeat this several times and notice how your feelings about meals begin to change. Write down the benefits of eating mindfully.

MINDFUL TOUCHES

Touch five things around you.

Use the sense of touch to connect you back "into the now." It is simple and powerful. It can be anything: what you are wearing; what you are standing/ sitting/lying on; parts of your own body; an item in your bag, or something around you. Slowly touch each item, focusing on how it feels under your fingers. Heighten your awareness by concentrating on touch only and blocking out your other senses as much as possible. As you do so, your breathing will deepen and relax. Your sense of touch will ground you in the present and give you a calm feeling. Make notes about how being mindful of what you touch affects you.

The next time a noisy environment affects you, calm yourself by detaching the sounds you are hearing and focusing on them individually.

When you home in on just one element, you will find you can start to disengage from the others. For instance, if you hear music and people talking, concentrate on just the music for a moment. Then transfer your awareness to one voice. By identifying them as separate sounds, it helps to ground and focus you. Then you will have the ability to focus on the sound you find most helpful or least disruptive. Note down what you found easiest to concentrate upon and what you found most difficult. If you find this useful, you may wish to try the suggestion on the next page...

NOISE AWARENESS 2:
Withdraw from unwelcome noise through mindfulness.

If you are feeling stressed by noise pollution and needing to calm yourself, try this. Focus on your breathing first, to calm and ground yourself. Observe each in and out breath for a few moments, and then take your attention into your own body. Feel your heart beating in your chest. It's a gentle constant rhythm that also has a sound. Allow yourself to hear the sound, a soft dum-dum. You can hear this more easily by blocking your ears with your fingers. As you slowly bring all your attention to the comforting beat of your heart, the other sounds around you start to recede into the distance, until all you can hear is your own heart. When you are ready, unblock your ears and slowly focus on the external sounds around you again. How did this exercise make you feel?

TWO

CLEAN A ROOM MINDFULLY.

This means doing it slowly, appreciating each item as you dust/polish/clean it. Ask yourself how you feel about these items and what they all mean to you. Notice what emotions come up as you handle each one. Appreciate your physical ability to clean: to bend and stretch, to apply pressure, possibly to move furniture. Enjoy moving your muscles and feel them enjoying the activity. Notice the different energy of the room when you have finished. Describe how both you and the room feel afterward in your journal.

Visualizing something solid and heavy helps bring your energy back into the present and lets you connect with the earth again. To make it even more powerful, imagine you have big roots growing out of the soles of your feet and that they reach deep into the ground. Notice how much more "in the now" you feel suddenly and write down any thoughts. It's normal if your feet feel heavier than usual for a little while!

Breathe in the first word and notice how it makes you feel. Breathe it out. Breathe in the companion word beside it and then breathe it out. Notice the difference between the two words. Repeat or try another word. Make notes about the sensations you have and where you feel them. Finish by breathing in all the first words only in the list.

Love/Hate ◦ Kind/Cruel ◦ Success/Failure ◦ Positive/Negative

Walk around it slowly, noticing how it makes you feel. What do you connect with most: the subject, the material(s), the color, shape, or texture? Or does the emotion or mood of the piece affect you more? What do you like most about it? What, if anything, unsettles you? Why? What would you think about having it in your home? What is the overall "message" you receive from the sculpture? How does that make you feel? What would you like to say to the artist if you could speak to them?

MAKE A CONSCIOUS DECISION TO MINIMIZE ALL NOISE AROUND YOU FOR A PERIOD OF TIME.

Turn off whatever you can. Then notice what less noise means to you and how it makes you feel. What do you miss, if anything? Check what you need or want to turn back on afterward and observe the effect it has on you. Think about every sound you choose to have around you each day and experiment with having less or more for a few days. How do silence and sound affect your ability to be mindful?

TOUCH A PART OF YOUR BODY TO REMIND YOU TO BE MINDFUL.

As mentioned in the Introduction, our minds spend a lot of time in the past or future, so staying mindfully "in the now" can be difficult. You can use a simple technique such as touching/tapping a part of your body to keep bringing yourself back into the present. It helps if it's something you look at often, such as a part of your hand or arm. It's also useful if it's a sensitive part of you that is pleasant to touch gently, such as the inside of your wrist or the side of your thumb. Experiment by touching parts of your hands and arms. What makes you feel totally present and aware? Notice how the touch immediately brings your thoughts and senses back to the present. Some people find it helps to touch part of their face or neck instead, or their legs. Work out what is most helpful for you and record your discoveries.

Close your eyes and see that creature in your mind's eye. What specifically do you like about it? See it clearly, hear, and smell it. Imagine touching it. What does it feel like? What emotions are you experiencing as you focus on it? What would it feel like if you were this animal? How does this animal live mindfully? How could you imitate that? Write it down. When you have learned what you can from your chosen animal, wash its energy away and ground yourself by realizing your feet feel heavy on the ground. Use whatever you have learned from that animal in a helpful way through your day. Choose another animal and repeat the exercise when you can.

SMELL SOMETHING THAT HAS A STRONG ODOR AND THEN CLOSE YOUR EYES.

What is your first response to it? And where do you feel that in your body? What associations do you have with that scent? Why? What images come to mind? If it is edible, do you feel more or less inclined to eat it now? Why? Make notes as you experience all this. To help wash it away afterward, let your outbreath rush through your nostrils or mouth and feel the scent leaving you each time you do this.

ALLOW YOURSELF TO FEEL THE EMOTION YOU HAVE RIGHT NOW.

Mindfulness doesn't mean we have to be happy all the time; it means acknowledging how we feel in any given moment. We can spend a lot of time blocking how we really feel, for a whole host of reasons. Sometimes we have to "put on a brave face" and the more we do this, the less mindful we become of our true emotions. So find time to be true to your present emotion. Let yourself feel right now, knowing you have your waterfall/shower to wash away anything you don't want to hold onto. Record the emotions you were feeling and why you felt them, also noting if you felt them in a particular part of your body.

GIVE YOUR HANDS SOME MINDFUL ATTENTION.

Our hands perform countless tasks through each day; how often do we stop to appreciate them? If you can't afford a hand massage or manicure, give them some loving yourself. Soak them in a bowl of warm water. Let all the parts of your hands relax and notice how good that feels! Pat them dry carefully and slowly, and then rub cream into them. (If you don't have any cream, a few drops of olive oil work would work well!) Really take your time, massaging each joint gently. If you study your hands as you do this, you will probably notice all sorts of things about them you haven't appreciated before, including how different parts of them are very sensitive. Enjoy your pampering and then notice how your hands feel afterward. Write down your thoughts on hand pampering at the end of your day.

What do you notice now you are looking at it in a different way? Try doing this with different things. Ask yourself how you feel about seeing things from a new angle. What else in your life could benefit from a fresh perspective? Make sure to write down your thoughts on what you discover.

JUST "BE" WITH A BODY OF WATER.

Water seems to have a profound effect on our sense of well-being—perhaps because the human body is made up of so much of it. Find time to be by a natural body of water: sea, lake, river, or even a trickling brook. Walk along it, immerse yourself in it, or simply stand/sit and "be" with it. How does it make you feel? Where do you feel it? Some people have a great need to live by water or to spend a lot of time on it or in it. How does that thought make you feel?

WHEN YOU NOTICE A BRUISE OR ABRASION ON YOUR SKIN,
STOP AND CONSIDER IT.

How did it happen? Why did you not notice it at the time? How often do you bang yourself and not realize it?

If it happens frequently, this indicates your mind and body may often be disconnected. What could you do to make stronger, mindful connections with your physical actions? Make notes on how often you discover bruises and when they might be occurring.

FIND A LOCATION THAT IS AS DARK AS POSSIBLE.

Sit in the darkness and notice how it makes you feel. Where in your body do you feel these emotions? What images, if any, come to you in the dark? Let the feeling of the darkness wash over and through you, and observe how it makes you feel. Notice how other senses become heightened as a result. Move back into the light gradually since it will feel brighter than usual after the dark. Take time to record your thoughts on this experience.

How much of the day is focused on you; how much on others?

What do you think about that balance? If need be, how could you balance it better? As you make your notes, reflect on the balance between self needs and needs of others, and what feels appropriate for you.

CANDLE 1:

Light a candle and gaze at the flame.

As you do so, take your awareness to your breathing, noticing each breath in and out. After a few moments, transfer all your attention to the flame. Focus on the colors, on its movement, how it makes you feel. Realize how beautiful it is. Reflect upon light and how important it is to our world. How is candlelight different from other forms of light? What thoughts run through your mind as you enjoy the flame? Write them all down. Try the suggestion on the next page if you feel comfortable.

CANDLE 2:

Light a candle and gaze at the flame.

Really study it closely and block out anything else around you. Feel yourself connect with the flame and its energy. How does the energy feel? Where does it resonate in your body? When you are ready, imagine the energy of the flame transferring itself to the part of your body where you feel the connection. See it literally moving into your body or feel its energy coming like a wave of light into you. Feel it warm and energize you. Notice what emotions it creates. Wash away anything you don't want. Remember to ground yourself and extinguish the candle flame safely before you continue your day. If you feel comfortable, let the energy of the flame stay within you for the rest of the day and notice how you feel as a result. Jot down your experiences at the end of the day.

PINCH YOURSELF (BUT NOT TOO HARD!).

What does the effect of mild pain do to your senses? What was your first response? Where do you feel the discomfort?

Notice what images come to your mind. Reflect on your relationship to health and being pain free, as opposed to being in discomfort. How often do you notice when you are pain free? How frequently do you feel gratitude for your health? Gently rub where you pinched yourself and feel the discomfort fade into nothingness. Record your answers.

If you feel life is overwhelming you, or simply that you need to slow down, counting is an effective mindfulness tool. Sit or stand comfortably with both your feet flat on the floor. As you breathe in and out, say these numbers silently to yourself.

IN: One ○ OUT: Two ○ IN: Three ○ OUT: Four ○ IN: Five ○ OUT: Six

Continue, counting as high as you wish. It will gradually slow your breathing—and your thoughts—and help you to feel calmer. Don't be surprised if you end up feeling a little sleepy and wanting to yawn! Record your emotions when you finish.

TAKE A WALK. WALKING IS A WONDERFUL WAY TO EXPERIENCE MINDFULNESS.
YOU CAN DO IT INSIDE OR OUTSIDE. WALK CAREFULLY AND DELIBERATELY,
AWARE OF THE SURFACE BENEATH YOUR FEET AND HOW IT FEELS.

As you do so, consider this beautiful, mindful expression by Thich Nhat Hanh:

Walk as if you are kissing the earth with your feet.

Try to walk that way. How does it make you feel?

SET A SOUND ON YOUR PHONE OR COMPUTER TO
REMIND YOU TO BE MINDFUL.

Because we tend to get sidetracked by the challenges of modern living, it is easy to forget our mindful behavior. A pleasant sound reminder can be useful. When it goes off, it takes you back "into the now" quickly and reminds you not to focus on past or future events. Choose a sound you find pleasant and uplifting. Then try another sound and see how it makes you feel. Jot down your discoveries.

CLOSE YOUR EYES AND PICTURE THE WORD "MINDFULNESS" IN FRONT OF YOU. WRITE IT IN YOUR IMAGINATION IF THAT HELPS.

Keeping your eyes closed, let the word pulse in front of you. It might even dance or move in some way. What is it trying to tell you? What is your relationship with mindfulness right now? How does that make you feel? You might want to imagine eating the word: What does it taste like? Absorb it into you; imagine it is dissolving into your body. How does that make you feel? Where do you feel the word most in your body? Why do you think that is? Write down your experiences. (You may want to return to this suggestion a few times and notice how your experiences change.)

EXERCISE VIGOROUSLY FOR A FEW MINUTES, PROVIDED IT IS SAFE FOR YOU TO DO SO.

When we feel sluggish, a great way to bring ourselves into the present again is to connect with our body through exercise. Just two minutes will help. Go for a fast walk, run up and down the stairs a few times, or do star jumps! The difference is immediate and makes you feel alive and grounded again. It is better to exercise briefly and frequently, than to find the time pressure of a longer workout means you end up doing nothing. Write down some easy exercises to incorporate into your regular daily life and make notes on how you feel after doing them.

CLEAN YOUR TEETH MINDFULLY. THIS IS A TASK WE HAVE TO DO FREQUENTLY, SO WHY NOT ENJOY IT? TRY TAKING YOUR TIME WITH EACH ASPECT.

Look at your toothbrush carefully; what condition is it in? Do you like the color and the shape? Pick up your toothpaste—what is in it? What made you choose this brand? Put the paste carefully on the toothbrush and then start brushing your teeth. Become aware of how your mouth really feels, its shape, and size. What does the paste feel and taste like? Where do you feel most of the taste and other sensations? How is each tooth feeling? Gently brush each one individually. Don't rush it. Brush the toothbrush along your tongue—how does it feel and taste? Focus on the feeling of water as you rinse your mouth. Run your tongue or fingers along your teeth and gums. How do they feel? What do you think of mindful teeth cleaning? You might be surprised by how much you want to write down after this simple exercise!

Close your eyes, breathe comfortably, and focus on each in and out breath. After a while, as your breathing deepens naturally, you may feel sensations around your navel, or through your hand and arm. You might see images or feel strong emotions. Describe what these are below. Just let yourself relax with whatever is happening, without trying to analyze anything. Feel the freedom of allowing everything to wash over and through you. Use your waterfall/shower if you need to get rid of anything unwanted. Take your time and don't rush this experience. When you are ready, take your hand away from your navel. Focus on your breath and have a final cleanse before you open your eyes. Then make sure you feel grounded, and your feet feel solid on the floor, as you write your notes.

CONSIDER EACH ITEM OF CLOTHING AS YOU GET DRESSED. RATHER THAN THROWING ON YOUR CLOTHES QUICKLY, LOOK AT EACH ONE FIRST.

Where did you get it? What was involved in its manufacture? Do you know WHERE it was made? What do you know about that country? How did it get to where you are now? How much do you like wearing it? How comfortable is it? What thought did you give before acquiring it? After doing this with each item, notice how you feel as you put it on. Once you are fully dressed, consider how much work/effort has gone into your whole outfit from a variety of sources. Give thanks for how you got everything as you record your thoughts.

COMMIT TO A CONVERSATION WITH SOMEONE YOU FIND CHALLENGING. YOU KNOW THOSE PEOPLE WE WANT TO AVOID BECAUSE WE FIND THEM TEDIOUS OR DIFFICULT?

Choose to give one of them your full attention. Try to let go of your judgment or irritation and focus on them as if you have never really seen them properly before. Perhaps you haven't! Tell yourself you will fully engage with them. Then do so. Listen intently to what they are saying, even if only for a few minutes. What shifts for you—and them—as a result? Record the outcomes as you repeat this exercise with other people.

Really dig your fingers into it and lift up the soil. Let it run between your
fingers. Sniff it. Cup it in your palms; focus intently on how it feels. Think
about all the soil on our planet. It covers much of the surface and is up
to six feet in depth. How often, if at all, do you garden and spend time
digging? Write down how thinking about all this makes you feel.

Why do you dislike this part of your body?
What is it you struggle to accept?

Now consider that part of you and what it does on a daily basis. How does it nurture/support/help you? How often do you appreciate it? What would have to happen for you to learn to like it? Close your eyes, focus on your breathing, and let yourself relax. Then take your attention to that part of your body and ask it what you could do to change your attitude. Observe what happens. Notice what you think and feel. Wash away any emotion you don't want at the end and make sure your feet feel heavy and solid on the ground before you make notes about your experience.

CHOOSE TO SPEAK MINDFULLY FOR A PERIOD OF TIME.
THIS MEANS TO REALLY CONSIDER EVERY WORD YOU SAY AND HOW YOU SAY IT.

What words do you use a lot? Why?

Notice which words nurture and which have a less pleasant energy. Which do you use most? What words would you like to use more or less after this experience? Write them all down and consider their impact on you and others around you.

Hold this position for a few moments, noticing the tension running up through your fingers, hands, and arms, before traveling to your shoulders and, finally, your neck and head. Release them and feel the relaxation spread through your body. Repeat several times. Appreciate how many muscles are used in this simple movement and how you can feel many of them when you are mindful. Give your arms and hands a little shake afterward. Notice if your energy has improved. How did that feel? Repeat when it's useful to do so.

For instance, what if all apples suddenly became banana-shaped and all bananas became apple-shaped? How would that make you feel and think? What other aspects of your life do you see only in one way—and what would happen if you chose to see them differently? What COULD you choose to see differently right now? Write down your conclusions and then return to this exercise a few days from now. What has changed?

Stop, sit down, and close your eyes. Notice how your body is feeling: frustrated, worried, or anxious? You might be feeling angry with yourself. Let those emotions wash away, using your cleansing waterfall/shower to do so. Now take your focus onto the lost object. Picture it clearly in your mind's eye. When did you have it or see it last? Where were you? Once you relax and focus, you may find you remember where it is—or even just "know" where it is without thinking about it too deeply. Good luck! Repeat this every time you misplace something and record how many items you find.

LIE ON YOUR BACK AND LOOK UP AT THE SKY.

What can you see? What do you know about the universe?
What would you like to know?

Keep breathing comfortably and gazing up, allowing feelings to wash over and through you. (If you find yourself wanting to look up more information about the universe afterward, that's great!) Write down your thoughts on the universe and how you visualize your place in it.

DECIDE YOU WILL BE KIND TO YOURSELF ALL DAY.

Have a day when you don't criticize yourself—or at least stop yourself if you do. Try not to put yourself under extra stress, either physically, emotionally, mentally, or spiritually. Keep the mantra "I am kind to myself" in your head all the time, saying it silently to yourself throughout the day. Observe how you feel as a result.

Find a store with testers of aromatherapy oils and delve into this scented world to see how you feel about it. What are you drawn to and what do you not like so much? Where in your body are you reacting to the scents? Learn about the different properties of each oil and see how you respond to that additional information. If possible, purchase one or two to experiment with them. Observe what oil makes you feel grounded and what makes you feel more light-headed. Which do you prefer? Which do you need most? Record how your mood changes when you use different oils.

Instead of deciding what those nice things are going to be, simply spend the day being mindful of the opportunities for this to happen, using all your senses to stay alert to positive energies. Notice how many occur as a result. Make a note of what happens—both expected and unexpected—and how you react.

Notice how you are feeling. Where is that emotion in your body? Why do you feel that way? Focus on your breathing for a moment. What made you drop it? Slowly pick it up. Stay still for a moment. Focus again on your breathing. How do you feel now? Write down how this mindful reaction made you feel.

FOCUS ON A FLOWER YOU LIKE.

Have a real one in front of you or close your eyes and imagine the flower in your mind. Why do you like this particular flower? What does it mean to you? Observe or imagine the scent, color, shape, texture, feel. What does it do to your emotions? What effect might another flower have and why would it be different? If this suggestion appeals to you, spend time looking up the spiritual meaning of different flowers. You may find you are drawn to some of them for a reason. If you can have some around you on a daily basis, jot down notes on how they make you feel.

BODY SCAN 1: YOUR FEET

Take a mindful journey through your body.

I have divided this into six sections since you may not have time to do your whole body at once. Sit comfortably with both feet flat on the floor or lie flat with your legs stretched straight out. (If you are lying down, this series of exercises can be a wonderful way to send you off to sleep.) Close your eyes and focus on your breathing. Then take your attention to your left foot and explore it with your mind. How is it feeling? What are the pressure points where it is touching a surface? Wriggle your toes. How do they feel? Transfer your awareness to your right foot and see how it feels. Is it the same or different? Does each foot feel equally heavy? Now ask yourself what you think of your feet. Reflect upon how often you use them during each day and how you treat them. Notice your emotions. If you are able and want to do so, give them a stroke. How does that feel? What more could you do for them? Sit or lie back and feel your feet relaxing and sinking deeper into the surface they are resting upon. Enjoy the sensation of them being able to rest. Record later how this made you feel.

BODY SCAN 2: YOUR LEGS

Continue your mindful journey through your body.

Focus on your breathing for a while and then take your attention to your left leg. Allow your focus to wander up your whole leg, noticing how it feels. Is it relaxed or tense? Are muscles aching or comfortable? Take your time before you transfer your focus to your right leg. Explore how it feels. Think of all the bones, muscles, and ligaments in your legs and what they do each day. How do you feel about your legs? In what way do you care for them? Stroke them if you wish, before you allow them to relax again. Enjoy the sensation of them not having to work for you right now and being truly at rest. Notice how pleasantly heavy they feel. Record later how this made you feel.

BODY SCAN 3: YOUR HANDS

Continue your mindful journey through your body.

Take your attention to your breathing and then focus on your left hand. Wriggle it a little if you like. How supple/comfortable are the fingers? How relaxed or tense is your hand overall? Shift your attention to your right hand and repeat your exploration of how it is feeling. Think about all the tasks your hands have undertaken so far today. How do you feel about that? In what way do you nurture your hands? What more would you like to do for them? Stroke them if you wish and then let them relax back. Notice they feel heavy and soft now. Record later how this made you feel.

Continue your mindful journey through your body.

Breathe slowly and comfortably. Feel relaxed as you take your attention to your left arm and let your mind wander up the length of it from wrist to shoulder. How is it feeling? Notice every joint and muscle. Transfer your attention to your right arm now and explore every part of it. Now consider them both. What do they do for you each day? How many hours do they have to work? Run a finger along each arm slowly and carefully. What would you like to say to them? Let their weight sink into the surface upon which you're resting. Record later how this made you feel.

Continue your mindful journey through your body.

As you focus on your breathing, become aware of your chest moving and think of your lungs working underneath. Then think about the other vital organs nearby: heart, liver, and kidneys. How is each of them feeling? How often do you consider the work they do every day to keep you alive? How do you nurture them? How could you be kinder to them? Let your attention wander through your whole torso, aware of the complex and beautiful functions in this part of your body. Give thanks for them. Notice how this part of your body feels more comfortable and relaxed as you focus upon it. Record later how this made you feel.

Continue your mindful journey through your body.

Focus on your neck extending upward from your torso and notice how it feels. It is knotted or tense? Does it feel supple and relaxed? Then turn all your attention to your brain. Let your thoughts wander through it and think about everything it does. Imagine your breath sweeping through your brain, relaxing, and reenergizing it. When do you consciously decide your brain needs to rest? What do you do to enable that to happen? How often do you rest your brain? Let your head and neck sink into the place on which they are resting. Notice how heavy they feel. Place your hand gently on your neck and then around your head. Whisper thanks to them. Feel them relaxing. This completes your mindful body scan. Go back and record how each part of your body mindfulness made you feel. Notice particularly where some sensations were very strong and what that means to you.

THREE

What do you like most about it? What images does it conjure up for you? What do you think about the words the poet chose to use?

Now read it out loud to yourself, slowly and carefully, forming each word fully. What rhythm or beat do you find yourself taking as you speak the words? What do you think the poet meant as he/she wrote it? Write down your feelings. What other poetry would you like to read mindfully?

DECIDE TODAY IS THE DAY YOU WILL ONLY PRAISE YOURSELF.
WE CAN ALL BE QUICK TO CRITICIZE OR KNOCK OURSELVES, BUT HOW OFTEN
DO YOU REALLY ACKNOWLEDGE YOURSELF FOR EVERYTHING YOU DO WELL?

Choose to spend the day giving yourself a proverbial pat on the back for what you do well. Write a list of all the things you are good at, even the humblest things. The more you acknowledge yourself, the more you will realize you are great at lots of things. Observe how often self-criticism bubbles up and remember to squash it. Note how you feel at the end of the day. Repeat this exercise frequently if you can.

THE NEXT TIME YOU TAKE A FAMILIAR JOURNEY, DECIDE TO NOTICE EVERYTHING YOU CAN DURING IT. IT CAN BE A SHORT SHOPPING TRIP OR SOMEWHERE YOU GO FREQUENTLY.

When doing something we know well, we can go onto automatic pilot and retreat inside our own thoughts. So this time really look around you and be fully present. Who or what do you see that you hadn't noticed before? How does that make you feel? Write it down. Notice every aspect of what you are walking upon and how different surfaces make your body feel. Repeat this and you will discover you find something new each time, no matter how familiar your journey.

BE MINDFUL OF EVERYTHING YOU EAT ONE DAY.
MAKE A NOTE OF WHAT YOU PUT INTO YOUR BODY.

How does your body respond? Where can you feel that response: in your mouth, throat, stomach, bowels? What made you choose those items? What happens when you really stop to consider what you eat on a daily basis? Write detailed notes to make this a truly mindful experience.

There are so many fascinating things to learn when you start looking! Here are two examples:

- The Milky Way Galaxy in which we live is one among billions in space.

- All the galaxies, planets, and stars make up only approximately 4 percent of the universe.

How do the facts you uncover make you feel about your place in the universe? Notice the emotions this creates and where you feel them in your body.

CHALLENGE YOURSELF WHEN YOU FEEL STUCK WITH AN ATTITUDE TO SOMETHING.

We all have times when we feel unable to make changes
—what is it for you?

The next time you feel that way, stop and ask yourself why you feel the way you do. Breathe deeply. How does your attitude to it keep you rooted within the issue? What can you do about it? How can you change your attitude, if not the situation itself? What would that do for your emotions? Wash away anything you don't want to be left with afterward. Repeat this exercise and keep searching for new opportunities to shift your attitude by staying present, acknowledging how you feel, and knowing you have the choice to change it. Jot down your experiences and reread them from time to time to appreciate your progress.

Notice how it is making you feel and then focus on your breathing for a few moments, making sure both feet are planted firmly on the ground. Allow your breath to relax you. How is your body feeling now you are reflecting on your thoughts and emotions? You may choose to extend your awareness to what is happening around you—that is fine—or you may wish to stay focused on your own feelings. When you write down your experience later, ask yourself what other situations in your life would benefit from the same treatment?

TELL YOURSELF THAT YOUR EYES HAVE SPECIAL POWERS ALL DAY.

For one day you have super vision and can see everything much more clearly, more brightly, because you are so well focused. What do you experience? Record everything that appeared different as a result of this exercise. What would happen if you did this more often?

PUT ON A COAT OR SWEATER, USING YOUR OTHER ARM FIRST.

I know that sounds strange, but we usually choose the same arm to put into a sleeve first. Notice what you do normally and then reverse it. How weird does that feel?! (Some people can't do it at all in the beginning, so don't worry if you struggle.) It's a great way to give your brain a bit of a mindful wake-up call. Try doing this more often and notice how it makes you feel. Chart your progress to see when it starts to feel natural.

THE NEXT TIME YOU FEEL UNWELL OR JUST OUT OF SORTS, USE MINDFULNESS TO UNDERSTAND IT BETTER.

Close your eyes and focus on where you feel unwell or uncomfortable. Where are you feeling it in your body? What is the sensation like: sharp, dull, throbbing, or a solid ache? Does it have a color, shape, sound, texture, or even taste? Spend time understanding it. Keep your focus on the discomfort and ask what you need to do to help it. You may be surprised by the information you get. Try to follow through as much as possible. Write down where in your body you feel the discomfort and notice if it's different when you repeat this exercise. Record any patterns and keep finding ways to shift them.

PICK UP AN OBJECT YOU USE EVERY DAY AND REALLY STUDY IT.

Consider its function and how it helps you in your life. How often do you appreciate its presence? How often do you use it without thinking? Use it carefully and mindfully now. How could you appreciate it more and not take it for granted? What other objects are around you that you could treat in a similar fashion? Make a note of them.

LOOK PROPERLY INTO THE EYES OF EVERYONE WITH WHOM YOU INTERACT DURING THE DAY.

This might sound obvious, but often our glance can be fleeting or even nonexistent. Decide you will look everyone in the eyes, no matter how brief your connection. Notice how you feel. Notice how they react. How does the energy between you change as a result? How do you feel at the end of the day? You might be surprised by what you write on this page. It sounds simple and yet it can be so powerful.

FOCUS ON YOUR BREATHING FOR ONE MINUTE, ON TEN SEPARATE OCCASIONS DURING ONE DAY.

Notice how long one minute feels on each occasion; does it feel longer or shorter as your day progresses? Don't force the breath at any time; just observe how it feels. Notice how you feel at the end of that day. Repeat on other days when you can and record how you feel.

DANCE WHEN NO ONE IS WATCHING!

Physical movement is an important way to express ourselves and yet, if we aren't dancers or physically active in our jobs, we can ignore how crucial it is. Put on music or do it in silence. Dance the way you feel like dancing in that given moment. No movement is right or wrong, appealing, or ugly. Allow yourself to be how you want to be physically and enjoy the freedom. Notice how you feel afterward and write it down.

Walk slowly through all the plants, really looking at them all properly. Notice the smells, colors, and shapes. Stop whenever you feel like it, to look more closely at anything that appeals. Touch it gently. What do you feel? Make a note below of what appeals to you the most and then research the plants when you have the opportunity. You may find you are drawn to them for deeper reasons than you first realized. You may also discover you'd like to buy quite a few of them! If you have the means, buy one or two to have around you and notice how they make you feel.

WASH YOUR BODY IN THE BATH OR SHOWER IN A MINDFUL MANNER.

How often do you rush the experience of bathing?

Try taking your time, and slowly washing every part of you with appreciation and gratitude. Notice the scent of the soap/gel and the feel of it on your skin. Become aware of which parts of your body feel sensitive as you wash them and which parts have less sensation. Why is that? Dry yourself slowly and thoroughly. Note down how your body feels afterward.

COMPLIMENT EACH PERSON YOU MEET DURING THE DAY.

It can be something small: "I like your watch;" "You have a nice smile;" or "You are good at that." Observe anyone you struggle to compliment and ask yourself why. Notice if it becomes easier or more difficult to do. Pay attention to how everyone reacts and how that in turn makes you feel. Reflect on how your experiences go at the end of the day and make notes about each one.

Notice how it feels. Now rub your fingertips together lightly and quickly for at least ten seconds. (You can do your four fingers together and then your thumbs separately.) Touch the item again. How differently does it feel now? Experiment with other items around you. Record what happens and which fingers are particularly sensitive.

Try to understand where it comes from. When did this behavior start and why? When does it manifest itself most? Where do you feel it in your own body? Does it have a shape or color—or a sound or taste? Connect with this trait and allow yourself to feel the impact of it. How might it benefit you sometimes? How could you alter it if it doesn't? How could you counteract or change its presence with something else? What would it take for that to happen? How could you support yourself to help it change? At the end, reflect upon how your relationship has changed with this trait. Wash away anything you don't want with your shower/waterfall.

PAMPER YOUR FEET.

They do a lot of work for you every day! If you can't afford a professional treatment, soak them in a bowl of water and notice how that feels. Then dry them slowly and carefully before rubbing in some lotion. Focus on each part of your foot as you do this and enjoy the sensation. After doing this, sometimes it feels as though you are "walking on air!" Write down how your feet felt for the rest of the day and how mindful you were of them as a result.

WRITE A LETTER BY HAND TO YOURSELF.

It is important to write with a pen or pencil, not to type it. Tell yourself how you feel, what you like, what you wish you could change. Write neatly and carefully, taking your time as you form each letter deliberately. Notice how your thoughts slow down as you do this. Read it through afterward. What have you written that you weren't expecting? You may have strong emotions when you finish: Wash away what you don't want. You might want to keep the letter or destroy it. Whatever you feel is fine. Return to this exercise when you feel like it. Make notes below about what you wrote and how it made you feel.

EXPLORE THE WONDER OF NATURE MINDFULLY.

You don't have to walk among nature to appreciate it. Look up facts, either online or via books, nature programs, the library. There are many ways to increase your knowledge. The more you uncover, the more wondrous you begin to feel about nature and what it can do. Where do you feel that sense of amazement and appreciation? What stops you from feeling that way more often? Commit to having a moment of mindful appreciation for nature every day for the next week. Notice how it makes you feel.

When you really focus on what people say and how they say it, you can learn a lot. Absorb the sound of their voice, their tone, and cadence. How is it making you feel? Observe their body language. Does it match what they are saying? Check in with yourself about how you feel deep down, not your surface response. Put down any thoughts you have below and notice which people seem most authentic or inauthentic.

If you can allow yourself a whole day, that would be wonderful. If that feels too difficult, choose a smaller section of the day. Even an hour would be helpful. Monitor yourself and notice any time you start to speed up. Stop, breathe deeply, and make yourself slow down. How do you feel afterward? What emotions or sensations have you experienced through choosing to be more deliberate and thoughtful? What are the benefits?

Ask yourself if it is the color, texture, size, or shape you find appealing. If possible, pick it up and hold it. What are you feeling? Discover what you can about the properties of the stone and reflect whether it resonates for you. What would happen if you had that stone around you? Explore other stones and notice how differently they make you feel. Record how the various stones resonate with your energy.

THE NEXT TIME YOU FEEL A STRONG EMOTION, CLARIFY IT.

Give whatever you are feeling a shape, size, color, taste, sound—even make it a symbol or object if you wish. Notice what happens to that emotion as you clarify it. What can you do either to hold onto it for longer, or to release it quickly? Write down what you have discovered to help you when you feel that emotion in future. Remember you always have your waterfall/shower to use when you need it.

Spend a few minutes focusing on your breathing and then scan through your body asking yourself, as you do so, what part of your body most needs attention. You will find yourself stopping somewhere. Check out how it is feeling and ask yourself why. Then ask what you could do within your power to give it a treat. Follow it through and notice how all of you feels afterward. Return to this exercise and make notes about what part of your body most needs attention.

VISIT AN ART GALLERY AND FOCUS ON A PAINTING THAT DRAWS YOU IN.

Really study it closely and ask yourself what it is that appeals: the subject, colors, shapes, mood, the message? Take your time and move around it, studying it from different angles. How does that change your relationship with it? How would you feel about having it in your home? What would the painting say to you if it could speak? What do you think the painter would want to say to you? Repeat this with other paintings and make notes about each one.

Take a break from your day's activities and decide not to focus on anything stressful or serious. Sit or lie comfortably, close your eyes, and observe your breathing without trying to alter it in any way. Then give your mind permission to wander somewhere fun. Let it know it doesn't have to perform any task. It is free time: Just for enjoyment! What happens? How does it make you feel and where do you feel it? Give yourself more playful moments if you can.

Wash away any emotions you don't want. Really study your eye color and shape and what your eyes say about you. After a few minutes, say to yourself "I like you" or "I love you." Notice how your body feels when you do this. If it's too emotional, stop and wash away what you don't want under your waterfall/shower. The eyes are often called the "gateway to the soul," which may be why humans can sometimes struggle to look into each other's eyes for any length of time. It can be unnerving to discover it is difficult to look into your own eyes too. Don't worry if you find it hard at first. The more you do it, the more you will learn about yourself. This is a deep, mindful exercise, so don't push yourself and be gentle as you explore. Return to this exercise whenever you wish and notice the changes.

FOCUS ON THE SCENTS THAT SURROUND YOU ON A DAILY BASIS.
WHAT DO YOU LIKE MOST AND LEAST? WHY?
SCENTS OFTEN HOLD MEMORIES.

What memories help and uplift you; what have the opposite effect?
Work out how to minimize the smells that negatively affect you.
Here are a few options:

• Wash them away through using awareness of breath through your nostrils and breathing them out of you

• Replace the memory of a scent with another, more helpful memory

• Change the scent itself, or mask it through using a stronger scent

• Change your perfume/aftershave and notice how that makes you feel

• Have a scent you do like nearby and use that when you can.

As you explore the world of scents, make sure you keep notes of your reactions because they may change over time and it's useful to chart your mindful responses.

123

FOUR

Do you know where it goes in your body?

The next time you feel yourself tensing up, stop and focus on your breathing. Close your eyes and scan your body with your mind. Where do you feel the tension or ache? When you become aware, direct your breath to that area and imagine each outbreath carries to the spot that is tense and gradually relaxes it. The more mindful you become of your tension spots, the easier it is to disperse the tension. Make a list of where tension manifests itself and notice any patterns.

Pick it up and then close your eyes. Now eat it with your eyes closed. Eat slowly and carefully, chewing many times before you swallow. How is this different from keeping your eyes open? When you open your eyes again at the end, notice how your taste buds feel as you write down your experience.

DECIDE YOUR PRIORITIES FOR THE DAY AS YOU WAKE UP.

What do you really need to accomplish? What could wait or isn't truly important? Trying to fit too much into your day is a quick way to feel overwhelmed and insure that mindful moments are even harder to access. Focus on what needs to be done and avoid adding in extra tasks that aren't essential or nurturing. Notice how you feel once you make those decisions and then stick to them. Write down what you decided and how your day changed as a result.

Breathe deeply and comfortably. Imagine a gentle waft of love coming from your heart, traveling down your arm and through your hand to them/it. Think the word "gentle" as you do this. How does this feel? Our energies can be surprisingly powerful and if someone or something is unwell, they may be particularly sensitive to what is being offered. Notice how you feel afterward and wash away anything you don't want. Ground yourself by realizing how heavy your feet are on the ground. As you jot down your thoughts below, pay particular attention to any physical sensations you had as you tried this exercise.

Animals have a natural ability to be mindful, whatever they are doing, so we can learn a lot from watching them (apart from animals confined unnaturally in small spaces as they are likely to be stressed). You may not be able to go on a safari, but you could watch a nature program or take a walk in a park where dogs are being exercised. The way animals put all their focus into whatever they are doing, whether foraging, catching a ball, or eating, provides a great insight into what being mindful really looks and feels like. What can we learn from animals? Write down your thoughts.

ASK YOURSELF WHAT "BEING AWAKE" MEANS TO YOU.

Sometimes not being mindful is called "being asleep" because it is through mindfulness that all our senses are fully engaged, allowing us to experience all aspects of life. What keeps you fully engaged in life? What makes you feel most alive? How can you encourage more of that into your life? What turns you off? What makes you shut down? How can you reduce those moments? As you write the answers to these questions below, notice how they are making you feel.

When you block out external noise, you become more aware of the sounds within your body and that can help you to connect with it more fully. You will notice the peaceful rhythm of your heartbeat; other more subtle sounds become noticeable after a while. Explore this inner world of you and really enjoy it. It's a lovely way to reconnect! Write below the sounds in your body that you could hear and how that made you feel.

**MAKE A LIST OF EVERYTHING FOR WHICH YOU FEEL GRATEFUL:
FROM THE SMALLEST OF THINGS TO THE MOST CRUCIAL.**

Take your time and notice how the list grows, the more you really focus on what is good. Write for as long as you can and return to the list later to add to it. Once it feels complete, go through it and make a note in your mind to feel appreciation every time you experience something on the list. Allow the positive feelings to flood through you and fill you each time. Notice how you feel after doing this frequently.

Look up quotations about mindfulness or read through some of the quotes below. Which mean the most to you? Why? What makes them powerful? How can you embody them in your own life?

"The present moment is filled with joy and happiness. If you are attentive, you will see it."

(THICH NHAT HANH)

"Be happy in the moment, that's enough. Each moment is all we need, not more."

(MOTHER TERESA)

"The moment one gives close attention to anything, even a blade of grass, it becomes a mysterious, awesome, indescribably magnificent world in itself."

(HENRY MILLER)

"When you realize there is nothing lacking; the whole world belongs to you."

(LAO TZU)

"Begin doing what you want now. We are not living in eternity. We have only this moment, sparkling like a star in our hand—and melting like a snowflake."

(FRANCIS BACON 1561–1626)

COMMIT TO READING FOR A SPECIFIC PERIOD OF TIME.

Choose something you want to read and start to read slowly and carefully, keeping all your attention on the writing itself. Notice when your mind starts to wander or something else distracts you and gently pull your focus back to the writing. Concentrate on what the author is telling you as a reader and notice how it makes you feel. Observe how much your mind wanders during the time. Try this again and see if it becomes easier to do. What are the benefits of reading more mindfully?

Take your time as you consider this question. Focus on your breathing first and notice what answers come to you. Don't necessarily accept the first answer as it may be a "surface" response. Sit or lie in silence and then delve deeper inside you to see what happens. Notice any images, sounds, scents, or tastes that come to you. Consider, and write down, how you can incorporate more of what makes you happy into your everyday life.

This is surprisingly difficult to do. We do so many things mindlessly, rather than mindfully, and keeping all our attention on one task at a time can feel strange initially. If you find a day too much, choose a shorter period of time. Notice how you feel afterward and make notes about what tasks were easy to do mindfully and what you found more challenging. How could you make the latter easier to do in a mindful way?

TENSE AND RELAX INDIVIDUAL PARTS OF YOUR BODY TO INCREASE BODY MINDFULNESS.

Focus on one part of your body—such as your shoulders—and tense the muscles as much as possible for a few seconds. Release. Enjoy the feeling of relaxation that floods through them. Repeat twice. Notice how your body relaxes more each time. Give the area a little shake or pat afterward. Ask yourself what parts of your body hold most tension. Make a list of them and then commit to tensing and relaxing those muscles each day. Notice how your sense of well-being improves as a result.

FOCUS ON MINDFUL BREATHING USING HELPFUL WORDS.

Words have powerful energies and can help increase mindfulness. Focus on your breathing for a few minutes without trying to change it in any way. Then when you are ready, as you breathe in, say to yourself "relax." As you breathe out, say the word "calm." Repeat these words silently with each breath in and out. How do the words make you feel? Would you prefer to say other words? Try using anything that appeals, such as peace, love, warmth, joy—whatever you feel you need. Experiment and note your responses.

Make yourself think clearly. Why are you angry? Who are you really angry with? Focus on your breathing. Where are you feeling the anger in your body? How would you describe the sensation? How can you release it? Concentrate on your heartbeat. Is it too fast? Allow it to slow down through mindful breathing. Notice how your body relaxes more as you do this. Now ask yourself: How do you want to respond? Keep breathing deeply as, this time, you choose your reaction mindfully. Make notes below on the occasions this happens and observe if any patterns emerge. What can you do to prevent being angry in the first place?

CONSIDER A ROOM IN WHICH YOU SPEND A LOT OF TIME.

Breathe comfortably and deeply as you wander around it, really looking at everything it contains. What is essential and helps you? What is lovely and uplifts or nurtures you? What is less useful or appealing? Why do you have those items? Note down the pluses and minuses. If possible, consider removing anything that has a negative influence. Notice how the energy in the room changes as a result.

WHEN YOU FEEL STRESSED AND FIND IT DIFFICULT TO THINK CLEARLY, STOP AND TOUCH A RANDOM PART OF YOUR BODY.

It can be anywhere and, to be most effective, vary the spots you touch as this will quickly ground you. To start, you could try touching the base of your spine (your tailbone or coccyx) since that is considered a helpful place to bring yourself back "into the now." Breathe as you touch the spot and focus on it. You may be surprised to discover that your body suddenly seems heavy or you feel a "thump" in your energy as you bring yourself back to earth, so to speak. After a while you may notice yourself unconsciously touching the area that needs calming: your heart when it is racing, your head when your brain is overloading, your neck when it is stiff, and so on. You can do this quickly and easily anywhere, anytime. Make a list of the areas you decide to touch and which ones prove most helpful.

CALCULATE HOW MUCH OF YOUR DAY IS SPENT WITH TECHNOLOGY OR ELECTRONIC MEDIA.

This could be your computer, cellphone, tablet, or television/video games. How do you feel about the length of time this takes up? What else could you do with some of those minutes? How could you insure you have more mindful moments without these items in your life? Make notes below about what you decide and then notice how it affects you as you implement it.

TRY THIS FORM OF BREATHING TO INCREASE MINDFULNESS OF BREATH.

PLEASE NOTE YOU CAN ONLY DO THIS IF BOTH NOSTRILS ARE UNRESTRICTED.

- Close off your right nostril with your finger.

- Breathe through your left nostril to a count of two.

- Close both nostrils and hold your breath to a count of two.

- Open your right nostril and keep your left nostril closed.

- Breathe out through your right nostril to a count of two.

- Close both nostrils and hold your breath to a count of two.

- Repeat the steps above.

You can do this to a longer count when you feel comfortable.
It is wonderful for balancing and grounding you.

Write down how you felt before, during, and after this exercise.

CHOOSE ONE TASK TO DO MINDFULLY EVERY DAY FOR AT LEAST A WEEK.

Select one that you do daily and that you will have the time to do slowly and carefully. Notice how you feel as you approach this task each day and how you feel afterward. When the week is finished, consider continuing the behavior. What else would you like to do mindfully every day? Write down any tasks you think are doable and then notice if you manage to do them mindfully too—and how that makes you feel.

THINK OF A CREATURE YOU FIND UNINTERESTING OR UNAPPEALING AND USE MINDFULNESS TO SHIFT YOUR ATTITUDE.

Choose a simple creature, like a fly or ant, and ask yourself why you don't like it. Then find out what you can about them as a species by doing some research. What makes them interesting? What makes them unique? Commit to understanding them on a deeper level and keep asking yourself why you found them so unappealing initially. You will realize it is possible to find every creature interesting, when you understand them better. And, in the process, you often find some quality in yourself that you weren't aware of. Repeat this experience with other creatures and make notes about what you discover.

WATCH A MOVIE OR TELEVISION PROGRAM MINDFULLY.

How often do you sit in front of the television or a movie with half your mind on something else? How easily are you distracted? Commit to focusing only on the screen and what is happening. Be aware when your attention wanders and gently bring it back. How much more do you get from the program by watching it mindfully? This becomes more and more enjoyable, once you get the hang of it! Make notes of which programs you watch mindfully and which you find more difficult. What does that say about some of the programs you watch?

Did you know each lung contains approximately 30,000 bronchioles—they are like tiny branches—and at the end of all these branches are more than 300 million tiny sacs called alveoli? When we breathe deeply, we want as many as possible of those sacs to inflate and deflate. Have this image in mind next time you focus on your breathing. How does it help you to be more mindful of your breath? Write below any further facts you uncover and how they make you feel.

Sip your drink and look around you. Imagine you are an alien from another planet, trying to make sense of what you are seeing; have fun with this! What do you notice for the first time? What makes sense and what seems strange when you consider everything this way? Write your thoughts below as you experience your alien responses!

LOOK AT THE COLORS YOU HAVE AROUND YOU ON A DAILY BASIS.

This can include your surroundings—both indoors and outdoors—and even your clothing. What uplifts you? What do you find uninspiring? What could you change to improve how you feel? Deepen your understanding of how colors affect you by trying different colors of clothing and noticing how it makes you feel. Make a note of the new colors you try and what happens to you as a result.

WHAT SOUNDS ARE ALWAYS AROUND YOU?

Stop and really listen during the day to work out what you can hear. There are many sounds we take for granted, such as the hum of electricity or low-level street noise. What can you hear in different places? Make a note of them all and realize how much of your day has noise in it. Decide what affects you positively and what you find unhelpful.

Our head weighs approximately 10lbs—4.5 kilos—which is a lot to carry around all day. Think about how often you let it relax during the day, to ease your neck and shoulders. Find a few minutes during the day to do this and notice how it makes you feel.

Try doing a crossword slowly, breathing mindfully and taking your time with each clue. It becomes easier to think and helps clear distracting thoughts! People may think mindfulness slows you down, but sometimes it speeds up what you want to do because you are focusing properly. So notice and write it down if you complete a puzzle more quickly when you are mindful.

PRACTICE PHOTOGRAPHY.

Snapping photos is a great way to be mindful, particularly when you take your time. Find a subject you like, and then really focus on how the angle and distance affects what you want to express. Try different things as you allow all your attention to rest on the subject and its surroundings. When you look through the photos afterward, ask yourself which ones you are most drawn to and why. Jot down what makes them so appealing and continue experimenting. Enjoy it!

HOW OFTEN DO YOU THINK ABOUT WHERE WATER COMES FROM?

Think about all the different ways you enjoy water and how essential it is for all of life. How often are you mindful when using water? How could you appreciate it more?

Consider the fact below for a moment and notice how it makes you feel...

All the water on Earth is constantly recycled, which means some of the water you drink will have passed through a dinosaur!

CONNECT WITH THE ENERGY OF A PLANT.

This can be a houseplant or a plant outside. Gently touch it, noticing how it feels beneath your fingertips. Is the texture smooth or rough? What do you feel about its shape, color, and size? Does it smell? Holding a part of the plant gently, close your eyes and focus on your breathing. Feel your energy coming down your arm, through your hand, and onto the plant. Now try to draw some of the plant's energy up into you. What does the plant's energy feel like? What is it saying to you? Remember to ground yourself afterward, by noticing how heavy your feet feel on the ground, before you write down your thoughts.

DEEPEN YOUR BREATHING WITHOUT EFFORT.

Find some time to be alone. Either sit or lie and close your eyes. Focus on your breathing without trying to alter it in any way. After a few minutes, breathe in to a slow count of three. Breathe out to a slow count of three. Gradually increase it, so you are breathing in and out to a slow count of four, then five, then six. Without pushing yourself, let the count increase until you feel it is enough. Then slowly reduce the count, one by one. When you are back to three again, spend time noticing how heavy your body feels before you open your eyes. Focus on an object around you for a few moments before you stand up. Jot down how high you could count and see if you can reach a higher number when you practice again.

SING TO ENHANCE MINDFULNESS.

You don't have to be a good singer to enjoy the benefits of singing. Making sounds is a great way to connect with yourself—and no one needs to hear you, provided you can find somewhere to be alone. Try singing something very softly at first and then gradually increase the volume. Choose a tune you like or lyrics that resonate with you. Allow your emotion to be expressed through your singing; let your voice vibrate through your whole body and embrace how it feels. Remember no emotion is good or bad—it simply "is." Wash away what you don't want when you finish. Then record what songs you enjoyed most and try others in future.

ACCEPT WHERE YOU ARE RIGHT NOW.

As I mentioned in the beginning of this book, often we get caught up in striving for our goals, instead of realizing the journey itself is the most important. We can also find ourselves in situations that anger, hurt, or sadden us and that make us want to move forward as quickly as possible. The easiest way to handle those difficult times is to stop and say, "I accept where I am right now." That allows you to be in the present and to acknowledge your feelings: the true reflection of mindfulness! Then you have the choice to release or to hold on to those emotions as you move forward. There is always your shower/waterfall to help you cleanse and your mindful breathing to calm you. Use them often to make your mindful journey as enjoyable as possible.

I wish you many pleasant, mindful moments throughout your life.